Celtic
prayers

Celtic Prayers

Selected by Avery Brooke
from the collection of
Alexander Carmichael
with calligraphy by
Laurel Casazza

The Seabury Press   New York

1981
The Seabury Press
815 Second Avenue
New York, NY 10017

Printed in the United States of America

Library of Congress
Cataloging in Publication Data
Celtic prayers.
"Selections from Carmina gadelica, volume III"—
Verso t.p.
1. Prayers.   I. Brooke, Avery. II. Carmichael,
Alexander, 1832–1912.   III. Carmina gadelica.
BV245.C4   242'.8   81-5693
ISBN 0-8164-2333-4   AACR2

Alexander Carmichael was born in Scotland, on the
island of Lismore, in 1832. Although a civil
servant by profession, his lifelong vocation was the
recording and translating of Gaelic prayers, songs,
and stories from the Highlands and
Islands of Scotland.
Today Carmichael and his work are revered by scholars
of Gaelic and Celtic studies and by all who rejoice
that he was able to save words of such strength and
beauty from a vanishing culture.

A.B.

The prayers in this book were gathered in the Outer Hebrides by Alexander Carmichael at the turn of the century. They were known, and prayed, by heart by fishermen and crofters who had learned them at their parents' knees and they from their parents.

Celtic Christianity has a flavor, a way, and an emphasis of its own which is deeply rooted in history. In Gaul and England, Caesar subdued the pre-Christian culture, but the Romans never conquered Ireland. There, Celtic culture came to full flower. Governed by a complex system of druids, bards, and brehons (lawyers) and educated in schools of oral learning, the Celts left us a larger legacy than is commonly realized. Their art forms, still influential today, were captured in superb metal work, and many of their inventions are the forerunners of modern tools and devices.

Although the earliest years of Celtic Christianity are obscure, the strongest traditions focus on St. Patrick and the fifth century. Patrick was born in a Northern British town of Christian parents. Raiders captured and carried him into slavery in Ireland when he was seventeen years old. There, while tending the flocks and herds of his master, he had time to think and pray, and the Christian faith of his parents became his own. He escaped, trained for the Christian priesthood, and returned to convert Ireland.

A century later, St. Columba and twelve companions left Ireland in a coracle (a leather boat) and landed on Iona, an island in the Hebrides closer to the shore of Scotland than the Outer Hebrides featured in this book. From their monastery on Iona, Columba and his companions completed the conversion of Scotland started by St. Ninian. The early Christian Celts became some of the greatest missionaries of all time, sending missions to, among other places, France, Germany, Switzerland, Italy, and Russia. There is even serious argument that St. Brendan reached the New World.

Impressive as Celtic culture may have been, it was a tribal one. There were very few towns and no Roman roads. Perhaps it was for this reason that early Celtic Christianity placed so much emphasis on the monastic way. Picture, if you will, a land with few towns. Here and there, on shore or mountain, a monastery stands as a Christian center, while most of the people live in tribes, tending cattle, farming, and fishing. These scattered people developed a lay Christianity, an everyday Christianity for use in the midst of their homes and work. Unable to get to church easily, the people brought the church into their daily lives.

It is this emphasis, persisting in Celtic Christianity down through the ages, which shows up so strongly in the prayers collected by Alexander Carmichael. The Celts had prayers for practically everything. Prayer was interwoven into their lives in a fashion that made it almost impossible to separate work and worship. When the sun rose in the morning, men would bare their heads and pray, when the women lit the hearth fire, they prayed, and when the children dressed in the morning, they prayed. There were prayers for starting work and starting journeys, for tending cattle, sheep, and looms, for planting, harvesting, resting, sleeping, and dying.

One reads these prayers with a growing nostalgia for another time. We think, "*This* is how life should be." And we picture a pastoral life of hard work, peace, and beauty. The more I studied Celtic Christianity, and these prayers in particular, the more I wished to know about the people who prayed them and I began to look into their origins.

The majority of the prayers in this book were gathered in the Outer Hebrides. These are the most Western islands off the coast of Scotland; Lewis, Harris—of Harris Tweed fame— N. Uist, S. Uist, Benbecula, and Barra. Today they are stark, but beautiful. God's creation—rather than the stress and problems and feared catastrophies of life in the modern city and suburb—seems to predominate.

In my research I was struck first by the spiritual continuity. On the island of Lewis one may see the standing stones of Callanish, dating two or three thousand years before the birth of Christ. Yet Scottish Gaelic *today* still has a phrase which means "Are you going to church?" but when translated literally says, "Are you going to the stones? " Many old druidic customs were happily blessed into the Christian faith while some prayers ask protection from "every brownie and fairy woman," from "banshee, nymph, and waterwraith."

Obviously, the prayers gathered by Carmichael had ancient roots, but someone, sometime, must have first prayed them— even if traces of much older times remained. What kind of life brought forth these prayers of simplicity, beauty, and faith? Was it a life style related to ours only by nostalgia, or does it have something to teach us?

What I discovered was startling: until the present there has been practically no time in the history of the Outer Hebrides that has been the pastoral and peaceful period that seems to be reflected in the prayers. Here are a few bare facts:

Christianity came to the Outer Hebrides either with St. Columba from Iona—the Inner Hebrides—or from his immediate followers in the late sixth century or the early seventh century. But the Celts were not left undisturbed for long with their new found faith. A few years after Christianity's arrival in the Outer Hebrides, the islands were overrun by Viking pirates—long before raids began on the mainland. In the ninth century, serious Norse colonization began, but the islands were alternately left alone and invaded by opposing factions. In spite of this, the Norsemen in the Outer Hebrides were converted to Christianity.

Neither were the years that followed peaceful. To give one example: in 1097, Ingemund was sent from Norway to rule the Northern Hebrides. "The worse governor who ever mismanaged a colonial possession of Great Britain...was an angel compared to Ingemund....His men gave themselves up to revelry, robbery, and rape...."* Eventually, the inhabitants rebelled and slaughtered Ingemund and his retinue. The next year King Magnus of Norway took revenge, killing chiefs and people and burning houses and forests.

In the thirteenth century, the Hebrides finally became part of Scotland, but that did not bring peace either. The island chiefs now feuded fiercely among themselves, and stories of cruelties, betrayal, piracy, and slaughter abound for centuries. In addition, islands were taken away from this or that chief by the crown and awarded to those he chose with the purpose of bleeding them for profit. The islanders would rebel and drive out their new governors only to be subdued by new representatives of the crown. Chronicles of the thirteenth to the seventeenth centuries read like a nightmare as did the centuries before. And from the sixteenth century right into the twentieth, one messy and bitter religious disorder followed another. The last of these disorders was not too long before Carmichael collected the prayers: A strict Christian sect became dominant in the Islands. Old men were forced to break their fiddles, young people could no longer dance or sing at weddings. As a matter of fact, even today you can't take a ferry on Sunday in the Hebrides. On top of this, in the mid-nineteenth century came the Highland Clearances in which crofters were cruelly driven from their homes to make way for sheep farming.

*W. C. Mackenzie, *History of the Outer Hebrides* (Edinburgh: James Thin, The Mercat Press, 1974), p. 21.

How then, in God's name, could Alexander Carmichael have found these prayers showing such remarkable spiritual continuity and which seem to us to be so peaceful and full of faith?

I don't know. All I can say is that it commends them all the more. If the Christianity which the island Celts began practicing in the seventh century was strong enough to survive onslaught after onslaught for thirteen centuries, it is all the more able to have something to say to us today.

I have said that Celtic Christianity developed its own distinct emphases. I am not speaking now of the specific differences in practice—such as the date of Easter—which were resolved at the Synod of Whitby in 664, but of the more enduring characteristics of Celtic spirituality which are shown so clearly in the prayers in this book. The major characteristic of Celtic Christianity, and the one that I believe has the most to teach us today, is the Celt's emphasis on immanence. The doctrine of immanence refers to God's omnipresence in the universe. Immanence is related to pantheism, but it has a different meaning. Pantheism sees everything as God. Immanence sees God *in* everything. In you and me, in field and flower, in joy and pain. The Celts' sense of God's presence and power was so great because they saw God in everything, worshipped him through everything, and turned to him for aid and guidance in everything they did.

We tend today, with our sophistication and with our yearning for simpler times, to think that the Celts just *had* this faith. "Weren't they lucky," we say, "that they had it to sustain them in their trials?" But I have come to believe that it was not luck. It was practice.

We need to *practice* the presence of God. It takes a great deal of work to simply train ourselves to turn to God. The Celts taught themselves, and they taught their children, to turn to God almost constantly. And in this practice we have something that is—if we are willing to work at it—attainable today and may sustain us through good times and bad as it sustained the Celtic Christians so long ago.

Avery Brooke

Celtic prayers

God

to enfold me,
God
to surround me,
God
in my speaking,
God
in my thinking.

God
in my sleeping,
God
in my waking,
God
in my watching,
God
in my hoping.

God
in my life,
God
in my lips,
God
in my soul,
God
in my heart.

God
in my sufficing,
God
in my slumber,
God
in mine ever-living soul,
God
in mine eternity.

From the wife of Donald, son of Eòghan, crofter,
Bernera (Barra Head), Barra

The reciter said: I heard this from my mother, peace to her soul, when I was young, but a poor tiny little urchin out and in at the threshold, as lightsome and foolish as the birds of the air. Little heed I gave these things at the time, and little did I think that you would come, dear one, to seek them to-day, after four score years. My mother was talking to someone of the old ways and the baptism by the knee-woman, and though I was small and foolish at the time, I was keeping an ear on her talk. And this is what my dear mother said:

When the child comes into the world, the knee-woman puts three drops of water on the forehead of the poor little infant, who has come home to us from the bosom of the everlasting Father. And the woman does this in the name and in the reverence of the kind and powerful Trinity, and says thus:—

in name of
GOD,
in name of
JESUS,
in name of
SPIRIT,

the perfect three
of power.

The little drop of
the FATHER
On thy little forehead,
beloved one.

The little drop of
the SON
On thy little forehead,
beloved one.

The little drop of
the SPIRIT
On thy little forehead,
beloved one.

To aid thee,
to guard thee,
To shield thee,
to surround thee.

To keep thee from
the fays,
To shield thee from
the host.

To sain thee from
the Gnome,
To deliver thee from
the Spectre.

The little drop of
the THREE
to shield thee from
the sorrow.

The little drop of
the THREE
To fill thee with
Their pleasantness.

The little drop of
the THREE
To fill thee with
Their virtue.

The little
drop of the
THREE
to fill thee
with Their
virtue.

Old men in the Isles still uncover their heads when they first see the sun on coming out in the morning. They hum a hymn not easily caught up and not easily got from them. The following fragments were obtained from a man of ninety-nine years in the south end of South Uist, and from another in Mingulay, one of the outer isles of Barra.

The eye of the great God,
the eye of the
GOD of GLORY,
The eye of the King of hosts,
the eye of the
KING of the living,

Pouring upon us
at each time and season.
Pouring upon us
gently
and
generously.

GLORY
to thee, thou glorious sun

GLORY

to thee, thou sun, face of the God of life.

From Catherine Maclennan, née MacDonald,
crofter, Achadh nam Breac, Moydart

The woman said: My mother was always at work, by day helping my father on the croft, and by night at wool and at spinning, at night clothes and at day clothes for the family. My mother would be beseeching us to be careful in everything, to put value on time and to eschew idleness. If we were dilatory in putting on our clothes, and made an excuse for our prayers, my mother would say that God regarded heart and not speech, the mind and not the manner; and that we might clothe our souls with grace while clothing our bodies with raiment. My mother taught us what we should ask for in the prayer, as she heard it from her own mother, and as she again heard it from the one who was before her.

My mother would be asking us to sing our morning song to God as Mary's lark was singing it up in the clouds, and as Christ's mavis was singing it yonder in the tree, giving glory to the God of the creatures for the repose of the night, for the light of the day, and for the joy of life. She would tell us that every creature on the earth here below and in the ocean beneath and in the air above was giving glory to the great God of the creatures and the worlds, of the virtues and the blessings, and would we be dumb!

Thanks

to Thee, O God,
that I have risen to-day,
to the rising
of this life itself;
May it be
to Thine own glory,
O God of every gift,
And
to the glory
of my soul likewise.

O great God,
aid Thou my soul
with
the aiding of
Thine own mercy;
Even as
I clothe my body
with wool,
Cover Thou my soul
with the shadow
of
Thy wing.

help me

to avoid every sin,
and the source of
every sin to forsake;
And
as the mist scatters
on the crest
of the hills, XX
may
each ill haze clear
from my soul,
O GOD

be the eye of God be

the purpose of God be

the hand of God be

the shield of God be

the desire of God be

the bridle of God be

twixt me and each eye,

twixt me and each purpose,

twixt me and each hand,

twixt me and each shield,

twixt me and each desire,

twixt me and each bridle,

And no mouth can curse me.

Be the pain of Christ **be**

Be the love of Christ **be**

Be the dearness of Christ **be**

Be the kindness of Christ **be**

Be the wish of Christ **be**

Be the will of Christ **be**

twixt me and each pain,
twixt me and each love,
twixt me and each dearness,
twixt me and each kindness,
twixt me and each wish,
twixt me and each will.

And no venom can wound me.

Thou Michael of
militance,
Thou Michael of wounding,
Shield me from the grudge
Of ill-wishers this night,
Ill-wishers this night.

Thou Brigit of the kine,
Thou Brigit
of the mantles,
Shield me from the ban
Of the fairies of the knolls,
The fairies of the knolls.

Thou Mary of mildness,
Thou Mary
of honour
Succour me and shield me
With thy linen mantle,
With thy linen mantle.

Thou Christ of the trees,
Thou Christ
of the cross,
Snatch me from the snares
Of the spiteful ones of evil,
The spiteful ones of evil.

Thou Father of the waifs,
Thou Father of
the naked,
Draw me to the shelter-house
Of the savior of
the poor,
The savior of
the poor.

In name of
FATHER,
In name of
SON
In name of
SPIRIT,
Three in One!

Father cherish me,
Son cherish me,
Spirit cherish me,
Three all-kindly.

God make me holy,
Christ make me holy,
Spirit make me holy,

Three all-holy

Three aid my hope,
Three aid my love,
Three aid Mine eye,
and my knee from
stumbling,
My knee from
stumbling.

The reciter, Dugall MacAulay, cottar, Hacliet, Benbecula, said that he always said this little prayer, 'under my breath', when he went upon a journey, however short the distance, however small the matter of his errand. He learned it from his mother and from her sister, who lived with his mother. These two old women had innumerable hymns, songs, stories and fables, sayings and proverbs, full of wisdom and beauty, almost all of which died with them.

less

Bless to me, O God,
the earth beneath
my foot,
Bless to me, O God,
the path whereon
I go;
Bless to me, O God,
the thing of
my desire;

Thou Evermore of Evermore,
Bless Thou to me
my rest.

Bless to me the thing
wherewon is set
my mind,
Bless to me the thing
whereon is set
my love;
Bless to me the thing
whereon is set
my hope;

O Thou King of Kings,
Bless Thou to me
mine eye!

O holy

God of truth,

O loving
God of mercy,
Sign me from the Spells,
Sign me from the charms,
Compassionate
God of life;
forgiveness to me give,

In my
wanton talk,

In my
lying oath,

In my
foolish deed,

In my
empty speech.

As Thou wast before
at my life's
beginning,
Be Thou so again
At my journey's
end.

As Thou wast besides
at my soul's
shaping,
Father, be Thou too
at my journey's
close.....

Be with me at each time,

lying down

and

arising,

Be with me in sleep
Companioned by
dear ones.

Thou,
my soul's Healer,
Keep me at even,
Keep me at morning,
Keep me at
noon,

On rough course faring,
help and safeguard
My means this night.

I am

    tired,

        astray,

            and

                stumbling,

Shield thou me from
snare and sin.

My CHRIST!

My Christ!
my shield,
my encircler,
Each day, each night,
each light,
each dark.

My CHRIST!

My Christ!
my shield,
my encircler,
Each day,
each night,
Each light, each dark.
Be near me,
uphold me,
My treasure,
my triumph,

JESU,

Son of
Mary!
my helper,
my encircler,
Jesu, Son of David!
my strength everlasting
Jesu,
Son of Mary!
my helper,
my encircler,

JESU,

Son of David! my strength everlasting.

May God
free me from
every wickedness,
May God
free me from
every entrapment,
May God
free me from
every gully,
from every tortuous road,
from every
slough.

May God
open to me
every pass,
Christ
open to me
every narrow way,
Each soul of
holy man and woman
in heaven
Be preparing for me
my pathway.

O Angel

guardian
of my right hand,
attend thou me
this night,
Rescue thou me
in the battling floods,
Array me in thy linen,
for I am naked,
Succour me,
for I am feeble and
forlorn.

Steer thou
my coracle in the
crooked eddies,
guide thou
My step in gap and in pit,
guard thou me
in the
Treacherous turnings,
and save thou me
from the scaith of
the wicked,
save thou me
from scaith this night.

Drive thou from me
the taint of pollution,
Encompass thou me
till doom
from evil,
O kindly angel of
my right hand,
deliver thou me
from the wicked this night.

Deliver thou me
this night.

The Gospel of the God of life

to shelter thee, to aid thee,
Yea, the Gospel of
beloved Christ
The holy Gospel
of the Lord;
to keep thee
from all malice,
from every dole and
Dolour;
to keep thee
from all spite,
From evil eye and
anguish.

Thou shalt
travel thither,
thou shalt
travel hither,
Thou shalt travel
hill and headland,
Thou shalt travel
down, thou shalt
travel up,
Thou shalt travel
ocean and
narrow.

Christ Himself
is shepherd over thee,
Enfolding thee
on every side;
he
will not
forsake thee
hand or

foot,
Nor let evil come
anigh thee.

To sea-faring people like those of the Western Isles the light and guidance of the moon is a matter of much interest and importance, often indeed a matter of life or death. Sun, moon, and stars are all addressed for practical purposes. The moon was of more concern than the sun, for by day, whether the sun was visible or not, the people could thread their way through their intricate tortuous reefs and rocks, fords and channels. But they could not do this on a moonless night except at the peril of their lives. In the extemity of danger at sea an old man at the helm may be heard crooning to himself:

GLORY
Be to Thee
O GOD
OF LIFE,

for the guiding lamp
of ocean, ccc
Be Thine own hand
on my rudder's helm,
And Thy love
behind the billows.

She of my love is the
new moon
The God of life
illuming her;

Be mine a good purpose
Towards each creature
in the creation.

Be my prayer,
O God,
In accord with Thy
sanctifying;

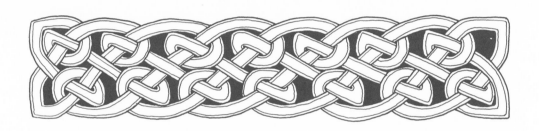

Be my heart, O God,
In accord with Thy
loving care!

Be my deed
on land
In accord with Thy
satisfying;

Be my wish on sea
In accord with Thy
directing.

Be my hope
on high
In accord with Thy
requiring;

Be my purpose below
In accord with Thy
satisfying.

From Peggy MacCormack, née MacDonald,
Aird Bhuidhe, Lock Boisdale, Uist

The reciter said that this and similar hymns used to be sung in her father's house at Airigh nam Ban in Uist. Crofters then held the land now occupied by sheep. The people were strong, healthy, and happy, and enjoyed life to the full in their simple homely ways. They had sheep and cattle, corn, potatoes, and poultry, milk, cheese, butter, and fish, all in sufficiency. They were good to the poor, kind to the stranger, and helpful to one another, and there was nothing amiss. There were pipers and fiddlers in almost every house, and the people sang and danced in summer time on the green grass without, and in winter time on the clay floor within.

'How we enjoyed ourselves in those far-away days—the old as much as the young. I often saw three and sometimes four generations dancing together on the green grass. Men and women of fourscore or more dancing with boys and girls of five. Those were the happy days and the happy nights, and there was neither sin nor sorrow in the world for us. The thought of those young days makes my old heart both glad and sad even at this distance of time. But the clearances came upon us, destroying all, turning our small crofts into big farms for the stranger, and turning our joy into misery, our gladness into bitterness, our blessing into blasphemy, and our Christianity into mockery.—O dear man, the tears come on my eyes when I think of all we suffered and of the sorrows, hardships, oppressions we came through.'

In Thy name, O Jesu
 Who wast crucified,
  I lie down to rest;

Watch Thou me
 in sleep remote,
  hold Thou me
   in Thy one hand;
Watch Thou me
 in sleep remote,
  hold Thou me
   in Thy one hand.

Bless me, O my Christ,
Be Thou my shield
protecting me,

Aid my steps in
the pitful swamp,
Lead Thou me
to the life eternal;
Aid my steps in
the pitful swamp,
Lead Thou me
to the life eternal.

Bless to me, O God,
the moon that is above me,
bless to me, O God,
the earth
that is beneath me,
bless to me, O God,
my wife
and my children,
and bless, O God,
myself
who have care of them.

Bless to me
my wife and my
children,

and bless, O God,
(myself
who have care
of them.

Bless, O God, the thing
on which
mine eye doth rest,
Bless, O God, the thing
on which
my hope doth rest,
Bless, O God, my reason
and
my purpose,
Bless, O bless Thou them,
Thou
God of life;

Bless, O God,
my reason and my
purpose,

Bless, O Bless
Thou them,
Thou God of life.

may God give blessing to the house that is here

May Jesus give blessing
To the house that
is here;

May Spirit give blessing
To the house that
is here;

May Three give blessing
To the house that
is here;

May Brigit give blessing
To the house that
is here;

May Michael give blessing
To the house that
is here;

May Mary give blessing
To the house that
is here;

May Columba give blessing
to the house that
is here;

Both crest and frame,
Both stone and
beam;

Both clay and wattle,
Both summit and
foundation;

Both window and timber,
Both foot and
head;

Both man and woman,
Both wife and
children;

Both young and old,
Both maiden and
youth;

Both warrior and poet,
Both clay and
beam;

Both gear and thong,
Both crook and
tie;

Both bairn and begetter,
Both wife and
children;

May the King of the elements
Be its help,
THE KING OF GLORY
have charge
of it;

Christ the beloved,
Son of Mary Virgin,
and
the gentle Spirit
Be pouring therein;

Michael, bright warrior,
King of the Angels,
Watch and ward it
With the POWER of
his sword;

Mary the fair and tender,
Be nigh the Hearth,
And
Columba kindly giving
benediction;

In fulfilment
of each promise

On those within,
On those
within!

Peace

between neighbours,
between kindred,
between lovers,

In love of
the King
of life.

peace between person
and person,

peace between wife
and husband,

peace between woman
and children,

The peace of Christ
above all
peace!

Bless, O

my face,
Let my face
bless every thing;

Bless, O Christ,
mine eye,
Let mine eye
bless all it
sees.